Basics of Environmental Method Development and Validation

William Lipps

Contents

ENVIRONMENTAL MEASUREMENTS

The purpose of an environmental measurement is to collect data that is technically sound and legally defensible. We do this by analyzing samples using standardized methods. Though we know that there is variability between individual labs that may run the method, we still assume the method gets roughly the same number no matter who runs it.

The method assumes the variability between reagents, calibration and calibration technique, analysts and instruments are small and controlled. Individual laboratory analysts rarely understand that the small modifications they make to a method may have a large impact on the data. Individual laboratories that make modifications compare the modified results to themselves or their own Quality Control (QC) criteria. Without comparing the results of the same samples with results of other labs, individual analysts may never recognize bias introduced by a modification.

Method developers often do not consider all the potential modifications individual laboratories may make. They assume the method will be followed. In addition, the method developer may not fully understand a method dependency on his reagents, reagent water, or specific technique.

When a measurement is made using an environmental method, the result needs to be trusted. How do we know it can be?

COUNTING AND MEASURING

It is important to know the difference between counting and measuring. The users of analytical data often do not. Counting provides an absolute number. Measuring is always an estimate.

If I have a stack of pennies, I can count them. If I count 100 pennies, I know I have 100 pennies. Easy. This is counting.

However, what if there are too many pennies to count? I will have to devise a measurement. Suppose I decide to weigh the pennies. If I know the weight per penny, I can calculate the number of pennies. This is measurement. Moreover, measurement is not without its complications. How much does a penny weigh? Well, that depends on the year. There is a maximum and minimum weight of pennies depending on the year they were made. I must get an average weight for pennies. The difference in weight per penny introduces error in my measurements.

How accurately do I need to weigh? If

only measuring a few pennies, I can weigh very accurately. Is this necessary, or not? The more accurately I weigh the pennies the higher my cost in determining how many pennies there are. I must compromise my measurement accuracy with cost of analysis. I need to estimate beforehand the acceptable error of my penny count. For example, is it OK to be plus or minus 10 pennies if I am measuring 100 pennies? Probably not. That is ten cents per every dollar. Accuracy to one cent, or one penny, is more acceptable. However, what about 1000 pennies. Now I need a bigger scale (balance). Here accuracy to ten pennies is 1%, the same as accuracy to one penny when measuring 100 pennies. A ten-cent error in weighing ten dollars is probably acceptable.

If we assume that the average weight per penny is 2.5 grams, then 1000 pennies weighs 2,500 grams. Our 10-penny accuracy requirement equals 25 grams. With a top loading balance, we could be much more accurate, with hardly any additional cost easily measuring 1000 pennies to less than the average weight of a penny (2.5 grams). However, as the number of pennies to estimate rises, the cost goes up. Either I need a better balance, or I need to repeat measurements in approximate 2,500-gram portions. If I tolerate a less expensive scale, I can still estimate the number of pennies, but cannot make the measurement with the high accuracy. The cost of measurement increases with the degree of accuracy required.

SMALL DATA SETS

If presented with a duplicate, a statistician will report the average difference may be 0.33 to 10 times the value of the data presented. The more duplicates, the faster the range tightens. Because of this, statisticians prefer large data sets. However, large data sets are rarely available. The good thing is that with scientific data there is usually a pattern to the distribution. If you have no choice but a small data set, collect measurements in sets of four. The average will be a satisfactory number. The only caveat is that these four measurements must be completely independent of each other.

In the normal law of error, most measurements will be close to the mean. Fewer measurements will be farther away. The average and the standard deviation define the distribution of results. Sixty - eight percent of the results are within one standard deviation. Ninety-five percent of the results are within two standard deviations, and ninety - nine percent of the results are within three standard deviations.

Different data sets may have different

averages, but they should have equivalent standard deviations; the average difference between duplicates is independent of the magnitude of the measurement. This allows you to "pool" information from different data sets, assuming analysis by the same method.

METHOD VALIDATION BY INSTRUMENT MANUFACTURERS

Method validation and the statistics used to demonstrate equivalency between two methods, or validation to prove the accuracy and precision of a new method is a very narrow topic. It is even narrower when considering the different types and uses of the potential analytical methods. Statisticians love large data sets. Data reviewers love large data sets. Regulatory agencies love large data sets. Unfortunately, large data sets are hard to come by considering the cost, and time required to validate a new test method.

Someone who has a financial interest in the new method undertakes most new method development. It may be a regulatory agency or an environmental laboratory attempting to solve a new problem, such as a requirement to analyze a new pollutant or to measure at lower detection limits. Most likely, however, a manufacturer looking for new markets for an existing, or newly invented, instrument or technique will fund method development and validation.

Manufacturers are for profit entities with limited resources to apply towards validation of new methods. While management may have dumped millions of dollars into the development of the new widget, they are not going to dump millions into proving the widget runs the method for which it was made. This sounds silly, but that is the way it is.

VALIDATED LABORATORY RESULTS

Analytical results are "validated" when a standard method, preferably developed using an inter-laboratory collaboration, is used. The laboratory compares its data to the acceptance criteria in the published standard method.

If there is no "validated" method, one may need to be developed. Standards Development Organizations develop Standard Test Methods. Often, the Standards Development Organizations are accredited by a national organization such as the American National Standards Institute (ANSI). In addition to accreditation, Standards Development Organizations may be recognized globally as International Standards or by the World Trade Organization.

A VALIDATED METHOD

A validated method should meet the following criteria:

- Published by a national or International Standards Development Organization
- Accuracy verified using Certified Reference Materials (CRM)
- Performance documented with proficiency tests

- Information on:
    - Specificity
    - Sensitivity
    - Bias
    - Limit of detection
    - Limit of quantitation
    - Precision
    - Linearity
    - Applicable matrices
    - Ruggedness
    - Within lab repeatability
    - Inter-laboratory comparison

VOLUNTARY CONSENSUS STANDARD ORGANIZATIONS

Manufacturers often go to voluntary consensus standard bodies (VCSB), such as *ASTM, ISO, AOAC* or *Standard Methods for the Examination of Water and Wastewater* to help create written standardized test procedures that use their new technique. Each organization has their own validation requirements, often written in documents only a statistician can understand. In addition, the validation procedure may be sufficient to satisfy the consensus organization, but regulatory agencies may not accept it. It is a difficult thing to spend thousands of dollars to validate a method that never attains regulatory agency approval.

Part of the problem is that the consensus standard organization volunteers almost exclusively focus on the inter-laboratory study as the method validation, or conversely they ignore the importance of validation. The inter-lab study is but a small part of method validation, much of which should occur as systematic steps during method development. The inter-lab study demonstrates, and documents, the between laboratory variability that occurs from differences in technique, reagents, and individual analysts. The inter-laboratory study does not measure accuracy, precision, selectivity, sensitivity, interferences, or "ruggedness". These should all be determined before starting the inter-laboratory study.

TERMINOLOGY

The nomenclature of methodology often varies depending on whom you ask. However, the hierarchy is defined as below:

> ➢ Technique – an instrument or scientific principle used to provide information
> ➢ Method – An adaption of a technique to a specific problem
> ➢ Procedure – Laboratory specific directions that follow a method
> ➢ Protocol – a set of instructions followed for method results to be acceptable

There are different kinds of methods:

> ➢ Absolute method – based entirely on chemical or physical properties
> ➢ Comparative Method – based on comparison of an instrument response with standards
> ➢ Standard Method – A method of known and demonstrated precision

issued by a recognized standards development organization
- ➢ Standard Reference Method – A standard method with known and demonstrated accuracy
- ➢ Trace Method – applicable to parts per million range
- ➢ Ultra Trace Method – applicable to parts per billion or lower

Expected Precision and Accuracy (P/A) of Trace Methods (parts per million)

% RSD	% Recovery	
0.01 -0.1	99 – 101	Highest P/A
0.1 – 1	95 - 105	High P/A
1 – 10	90 – 110	Intermediate P/A
10 – 35	85 - 115	Low P/A
>35	75 - 125	Semi quantitative

Expected Precision and Accuracy (P/A) of
Ultra Trace Methods (parts per billion or
less)

% RSD	% Recovery	
0.1 -1.0	95 - 105	Highest P/A
1 – 10	90 - 110	High P/A
10 - 35	85 – 115 (75 – 125)	Intermediate P/A
> 35	75 – 125 (70 – 130)	Low P/A

() organics

METHOD DEVELOPMENT IS A PROCESS

Another problem, and the reason for this writing, is that method developers (which may include product specialists and applications chemists at instrument manufacturers, and/or bench chemists at commercial or government labs) may not be familiar with method development process or statistics. As laboratory chemists, they may be familiar with validating existing analytical methods for use in their lab, but may not be familiar with establishing the validation criteria that must be included in each new method. These criteria may include detection limits, laboratory control sample recovery and precision limits, the calibration model and acceptance criteria, quantitation range, linear range, interferences, and acceptance criteria for matrix spikes and duplicates. A new method contains none of this data. The method developer creates it.

Finally, the developer must write the method in an unambiguous form. The new written method includes all reagents that must be prepared and how to prepare them. The method includes instructions for sampling, sample preservation, and holding time. If the new method analyzes a new parameter, there is no prerequisite. The method developer must establish these criteria using experimental data. Reagent shelf life and storage containers must be experimentally determined and documented. Each potential interference should be tested with and without the analyte present. Increasing concentrations of potential interferences are tested so the upper limit of an interference is known. Finally, the method developer determines ruggedness of the written method. In ruggedness testing, he tries to "break" the method changing various parameters he believes an analyst may modify. These can include, but are not limited to, sample weights or volumes, reagent weights, volumes, or storage times, extraction times, digestion temperatures or times, order of reagent addition, incubation times, and so forth. If any of these variables significantly affect sample results, write the method so that analysts do not modify important variables.

THE PURPOSE OF A METHOD

The purpose of following an established method is to reduce the variability of results between laboratories. Inside individual laboratories, the analyst cannot know whether his/her modification biased the results relative to laboratories that made no modification. Figure 1 is an example of a Youden two-sample plot used to evaluate method results from a collaborative study. Using Youden pairs, the lab runs blind duplicates that are almost, but not exactly the same concentration. These pairs are plotted as in Figure 1.

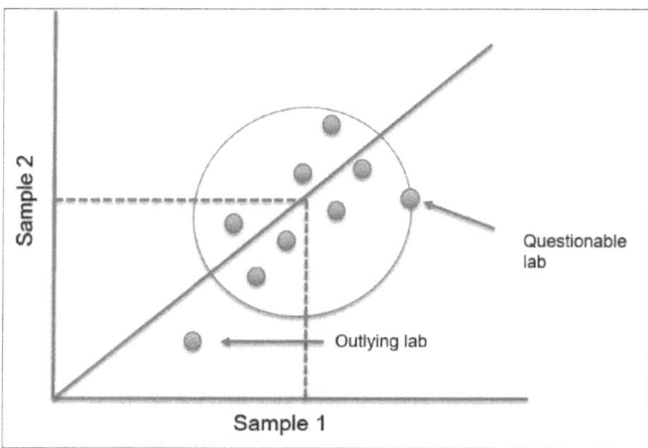

Figure 1 Youden Pairs of an Inter-laboratory Study

If only random error exists, the data points are distributed randomly around the intersection of the two means (Figure 2).

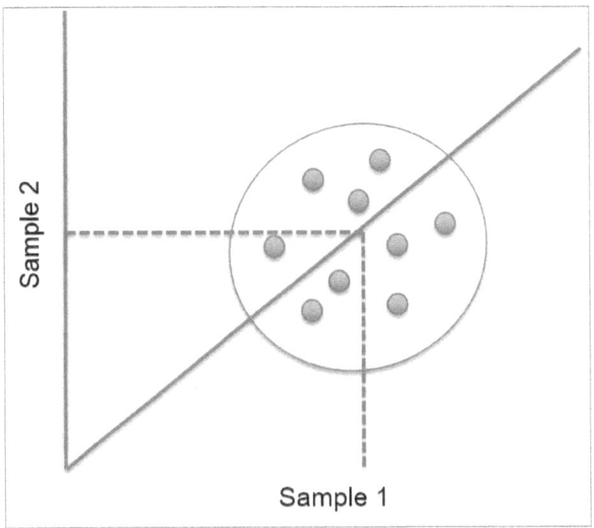

Figure 2 Unbiased data in a Youden Plot

The example in Figure 2 of unbiased data almost never happens. Instead, data is almost always distributed, as in Figure 1, along a 45-degree line intersecting the intersection of means. The distance away from the mean along this 45-degree line shows the systematic bias. This bias comes from small differences in laboratories in the way they calibrate, extract, dilute, or prepare standards. This systematic bias can only be detected by comparing your results with another lab. Only by following a well validated method, and not modifying certain parameters that the method developers discovered cannot be modified will the results from labs fall within reasonable precision and bias.; each time a modification is made, you don't know how your results will compare to other labs. Notice the outlying lab. Though the chart in Figure 1 is just an example, the outlier is included to show what would happen if a lab decided to modify a method and cause results to be low.

MODIFYING METHODS

Each method intends to measure something and produce a result of some value to a data user. Usually the result is a number. Most methods are rational methods, meaning two or more methods measuring the same thing will produce the same result within experimental error. A laboratory chooses a method based on available equipment and required sample throughput.

Empirical methods have some aspect in the method that defines the outcome. For example, if you modify the 5-day BOD to four or six days, the result could be different. Analytes of empirical methods are called Method Defined Parameters. Before modifying an empirical method first, determine what cannot be modified; and what part of the method is defined.

Sometimes we assume methods are empirical because nobody knew the true analyte during method development. An example is "available" cyanide. Later, with more experimentation and speciation, the exact metal cyanide complexes measured by the "available" cyanide methods were discovered.   Always try to define the exact analyte enabling you to re-define empirical methods as rational methods.

Take, for example, total phosphorus. Phosphorus is an element. There can be only one true concentration of phosphorus in a sample. Therefore, "total phosphorus" is not a method-defined parameter. If a new method digests and measures total phosphorus at a statistically lower concentration than another method, the new method is flawed.

Now, consider "hydrolysable" phosphorus. The digestion procedure defines the amount recovered. Modify the digestion procedure and you may change the result. The hydrolysable phosphorus digestion is method defined.

What about Total Kjeldahl Nitrogen, or TKN? At first glance, the results are considered method defined because the result is defined by the digestion procedure. However, the intent of the TKN test is to measure total nitrogen, and there are multiple digestions all under the umbrella of "TKN". Total nitrogen is a rational number; there is an absolute quantity of total nitrogen in a sample. Gauge new methods by their ability to determine total nitrogen and not by how well the results match TKN.

RE-WRITING A MODIFIED METHOD

Once you make a modification to a method, you must demonstrate that results are comparable to the original method in non-interfering samples. Necessary tests to demonstrate equivalence include the method detection limit (MDL), linearity, calibration range, accuracy/precision, and analysis of an independent quality control sample. Run all of these tests using both methods. Perform an equivalency test. This differs from a T-Test. The T-Test checks to see if the means are the same. The equivalency test assumes the means are the same and verifies that the variance is equal (Figure 3). It does this using a two-sided T-Test.

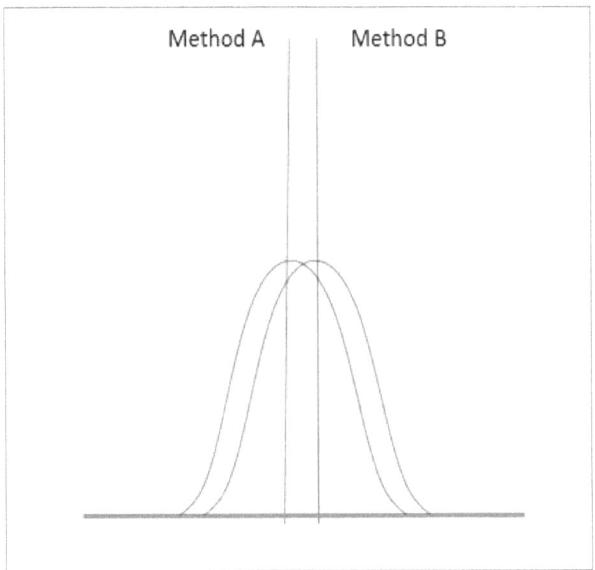

Figure 3 two nearly equivalent means with equivalent precision

Perform the Equivalence test using the concentration detected on the same samples run in multiple replicates over a period of several days. You have to run both the new method, and the old method. In addition, use at least three samples with concentrations that span the range of the method. The test should show equivalency at all concentrations.

Not all new methods have to be "equivalent", however. A new method may have better precision and still get the same result (Figure 4).

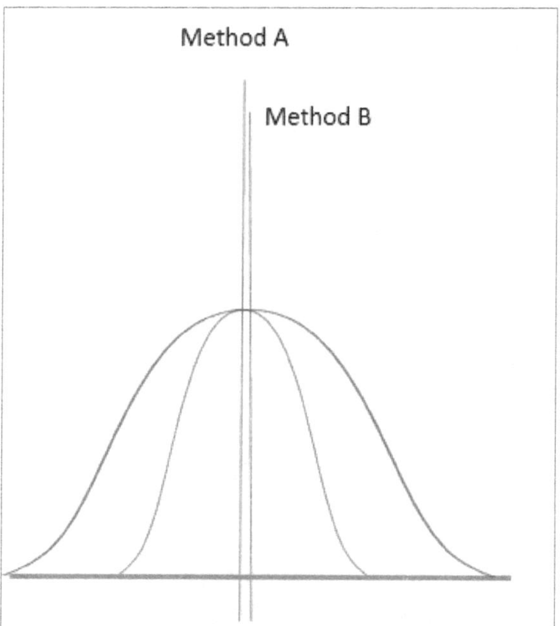

Figure 4 two methods with the same mean and different precision

Alternatively, the new method may have equivalent precision and get a different result (Figure 5).

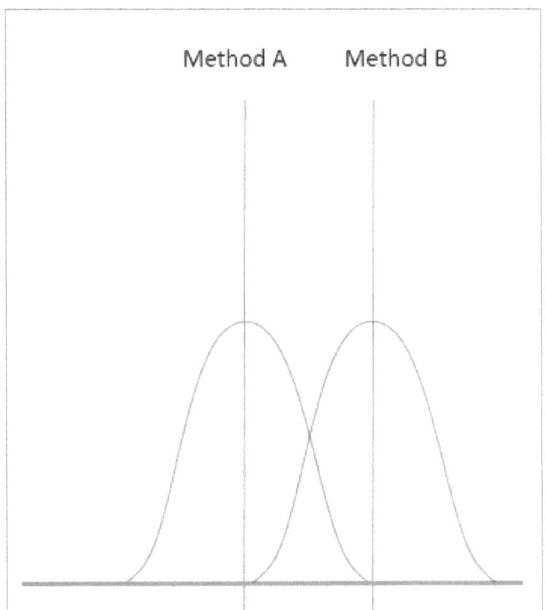

Figure 5 two methods with different means and the same precision

In this case, you must demonstrate that the results of the new method more accurately reflect the true concentration in the samples.

Some new methods may have better precision, but the means differ as in Figure 6. In this case, the mean of the new method is within the range of the old method. Statistical comparison fails both the F-Test and the T-Test; however, the mean of the new method is within the acceptance limits of the old method.

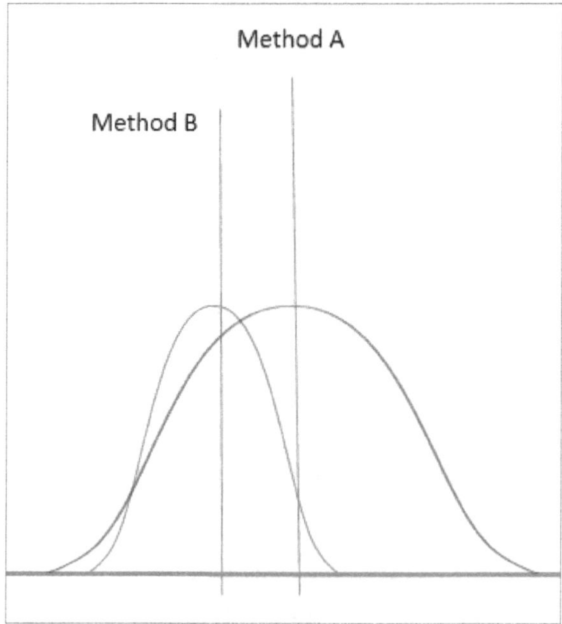

Figure 6 two methods with different means and different precision, however, the mean of Method B falls within the precision of Method A.

Measure accuracy and precision for the new method. The more replicates you do the better, so for accuracy and precision run 7 - 10 replicates of at least three concentrations spanning the range of the method.

Once you have compared the means and standard deviation of the modified method to the existing method in non-interfering samples, you now need to test in real matrices. If you know what compounds interfere with the original method, analyze a matrix with and without analyte containing the interference. Repeat the analyte concentrations used for the accuracy and precision test. Also, add the potential interference at various concentrations up to the concentration reasonably expected in samples. If no interference is evident, run 7 - 10 replicates and determine accuracy and precision with "interference" present. Repeat with all known interferences.

For new methods, you determine the mean and standard deviation in non-interfering matrices, and then test in real matrices. Using your knowledge of chemistry, estimate what compounds interfere, and analyze a matrix with and without analyte containing the interference. Repeat the analyte concentrations used for the accuracy and precision test. Also, add the potential interference at various concentrations up to the concentration reasonably expected in samples. If no interference is evident, run 7 - 10 replicates and determine accuracy and precision with "interference" present. Repeat with all suspected interferences.

Obtain up to nine representative matrices and analyze for the analyte. Spike known concentrations of analyte and run 7 - 10 replicates. Calculate accuracy and precision. Plot the expected concentration versus the found concentration of each matrix (Figure 7).

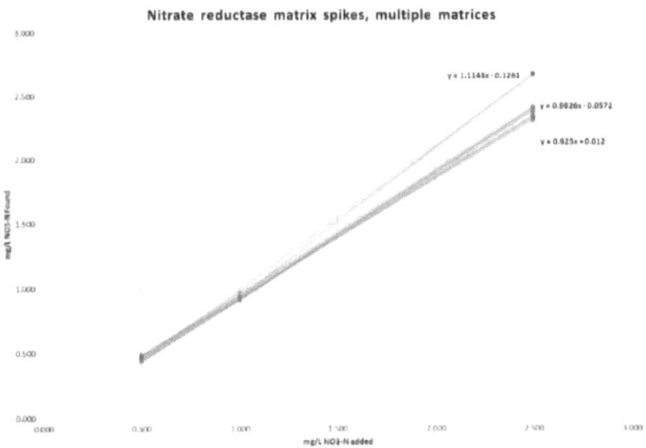

Figure 7 Eleven spiked matrices analyzed for nitrate

Visually examine the curves. They should all have similar slopes and intercepts. If necessary, obtain the equation of each line and perform a T Test on the slopes and intercepts to ensure data are the same. If one

curve is significantly different, that matrix
has an interference. Either limit the method
as not applicable to that matrix, or determine
the cause and correct the method. Keep in
mind that if you modify the method, you
must repeat all the previous validation steps.

SO YOU WANT TO MAKE A METHOD

Loosely defined, a method is a group of procedures including specifications of apparatus, instruments, reagents, operations to follow, and conditions so that you can make a measurement. When you carry out the instructions, you are following a measurement process. That process is the method. However, there is also a process for developing a method. You must carry out a series of well-designed experiments to describe the apparatus, specific conditions, reagents, and operations you need to complete before you can even sit down to write the first draft. As you follow these defined method development steps, recording your observations as you go, the method almost writes itself.

Before you start a method, you have to have an idea of what you want it to do. You may have a new instrument capable of measuring something for which there are no methods. You may have an improved technique, or apparatus, that will save people time, or reduce reagents and hazardous waste. You may have a new material for which you need a new analytical method. Whatever the reason, you have decided you need a new method.

Now, the first step is to write a clear and concise title. The title should describe the analyte (or group of analytes), the matrices, any digestion or extraction, and the determination technique. For example:

Determination of Iron in Iron Ore by Acid Dissolution and Titration with Dichromate

Better yet:

Determination of Iron in Siderite by Hydrochloric Acid Dissolution and Titration with Potassium Dichromate

With a well-defined title, you know what the method is about and what it is supposed to do. Define it even further with a scope. The scope includes the matrices the method is applicable to, the concentration range that can be accurately measured, and sometimes what the method is used for. The original scope is subject to change as you work to validate the method. For example, you may have included seawater in your original scope, and then decide later the method does not work with a seawater matrix so you remove it.

Once you have a title and a scope you can start a series of single laboratory experiments and use them to start writing the steps that will eventually become the method.

TITLE AND SCOPE AT CONSENSUS ORGANIZATIONS

At consensus standard organizations, such as *ASTM* or *Standard Methods*, a group of people called a task group, or a committee decide the title and scope. You propose the new method for development at the consensus organization and a committee decides if it is worthwhile for the organization to pursue method development. The organization will appoint a task group to work with you on the method. Often, unless you do not want the role, you will be appointed to head the task group. The task group members collectively agree upon and write the title and the scope.

PREVENTING METHOD CREEP

Defining a title and a scope early on helps prevent scope creep and keeps the development process on track. Using the title and scope makes it easier to write a method development plan. This plan includes extensive single lab studies that may consist of much "trial and error". Having a plan minimizes the "shotgun" approach and helps to uncover deficiencies that should be overcome prior to an inter-laboratory study. A bad method makes a bad, and expensive, inter-laboratory study.

The hardest part in coming up with a method development plan is you must know in advance what variables to test. It helps to look closely at these three components of all methods:

1) The sample matrices, preservation, and storage

2) The instrument or measuring device

3) Education level of the analyst

The complexity of the method development is limited by the scope. If the scope narrowly defines the sample type, then development is simplified. If the scope includes broad, poorly defined matrices, such as "wastewater", then method development and validation is complicated. You need to use your knowledge to "predict" potential interferences and test the procedure to ensure the method overcomes these potential interferences. Errors from interferences or variability in sample homogeneity, or loss of analyte during storage, outweigh measurement errors. A method may require hours of sample preparation for a 30 second reading on an instrument.

INSTRUMENTS AND STANDARD SOLUTIONS

Instruments must be adjusted, tuned if you will, so that day-to-day measurements are obtained under similar conditions. Standard solutions must be prepared and dispensed in the same way, and from scrupulously cleaned vessels.

Repeat standard preparation and instrument adjustment numerous times to ensure your procedures are repeatable.

ANALYSTS

Analysts can be tired, not feeling well, have periodic personal problems. These things can affect everything from sample and reagent preparation to the final measurement.

Use different analysts early in the development process having them follow the preliminary instructions. If the instructions fail, modify them. Attempt to write the instructions clearly enough that anybody can follow them. However, avoid being so specific (unless necessary) to prevent allowed modifications or differences in instruments and apparatus.

CALIBRATION

To determine, or estimate, the variables of a testing method requires a full understanding of the final measurement process. Validate the instrument and/or measurement step on pure standards first. To do this, you must determine which standards to use, and at what concentrations. What stabilizers, such as acid, should be included to ensure the analyte concentration does not change with storage? How do you verify enough stabilizer was added? What solvent should the standard be prepared in? What salts or organic compounds should you weigh? What is their minimum purity? What concentration should you make your stock? It needs to be high enough for accurate weighing and low enough for reasonable dilutions. It needs to be stable for as long as possible, within reason.

Once you determine the compounds, reagents, and technique to prepare your calibration curve, you must make the standards with highest accuracy needed for the test. Then estimate the concentrations needed for your new method and prepare the standards. Prepare a range of increasing concentration from as low as you think you can go to as high as you think possible by the technique. Analyze a mid-range standard and examine the response. Did you make standards in the right range? You may need to prepare more either higher or lower depending on this outcome. Now, aspirate/inject replicates of each standard recording the response. You need at least three replicates to verify the measurement is repeatable. Plot the average response versus concentration and check for linearity. Adjust your standards accordingly. Quadratic fitting is acceptable, but be cautious. A linear fit is the goal.

For chromatographic methods, you may spend a lot of time adjusting chromatographic conditions. These include, but are not limited to, flow rates, gradients (either temperature or reagent), injection volumes, liners, columns, detector, injector, temperatures, etc.

Conditions of the measurement, regardless of technique, need to be "optimized". Spend time making sure the measurement step is as good as it can get, within reason. Then calibrate as above. Repeat the calibration over a period of several days, making sure the calibration model holds for the calibration range chosen.

CALIBRATION SOLUTIONS

Determine the best, most efficient way to prepare standards. Verify the purity of neat solutions and check other manufacturers, suppliers, or lots to ensure there is nothing unique about yours. Document the solvent used and its purity. If the solvent is reagent water, document the conductivity and other trace components, if known.

Record exactly how to make the calibration standards, and repeat the preparation at least three times. Each of the times should result in responses that are statistically the same.

SHELF LIFE OF STANDARDS AND REAGENTS

Determine the shelf life of standards and reagents. Prepare a batch of each, and store in different containers, such as glass, high-density polyethylene (HDPE), low-density polyethylene (LDPE), and polypropylene. Store an aliquot of each at room temperature and one refrigerated. If the chemistry suggests light may be a factor, store an aliquot of the room temperature in the dark and one exposed to laboratory light. Monitor the response over time. Continue monitoring until you notice a significant change in response. If you already know the shelf life, such as 6 months for trace metals preserved with nitric acid, you can use this existing knowledge.

BLANKS

Run blanks of solvent or reagent water containing everything except the analyte. Look for contamination. If you detect contamination, find its source, and document so that other operators will know about them. If certain reagents are likely to contain the analyte, find a suitable grade, and warn analysts to purchase that grade. If no reagent completely free of analyte is available, find another suitable reagent, a work around, or instructions on how to purify the reagent to reduce contamination.

Once you are sure about shelf life, and reagent preparation, repeat the calibration verifying blanks are not detected or at a minimum. Analyze up to nine replicates each of the blank and each calibration standard. Remember that method blanks are carried through the entire process; they must go through all phases of sample preparation. Preferably, this would include adding blanks to storage/sampling containers, adding preservatives, storing up to the holding time, and analyzing as you would a sample.

If the lowest calibration standard is about three times the estimated method detection limit (MDL), calculate the MDL as 3.143 times the standard deviation of seven replicates of the lowest calibration standard. Calculate the mean and standard deviation of each set of replicates. Use this data to calculate average recovery and percent relative standard deviation.

BEGINNING THE SINGLE LABORATORY VALIDATION

The good news is that the single laboratory validation steps all follow the same pattern as the calibration development process. You will repeat what you have already done measuring repeatability and recovery of calibration standards on a series of matrices. This validates that the method not only works for standards, but also on samples/matrices tested. If you find a matrix where measurement of analyte fails, then you decide whether the method should be applicable to that matrix, or whether you should make a modification. If you make a modification, you need to repeat all the steps done to validate the calibration. If you modify a reagent, its preparation and storage validation needs to be repeated.

Remember to carry all matrices through the entire process; they must go through all phases of sample preparation. Preferably, this would include adding test matrices to storage/sampling containers, adding preservatives, storing up to the holding time, and analyzing as you would a sample.

SINGLE LAB VALIDATION ON MATRICES WITH ANALYTE PRESENT

Find representative matrices with concentrations near the lowest point of the calibration curve, one near the middle of the curve, and one near the top of the curve. Split each matrix into two portions. Dilute one aliquot of each portion by 20%, so that its concentration is 80% of the other half. Calibrate the method according to the new method instructions and analyze nine replicates of each portion of each digested/extracted matrix. Do three replicates on one day, three replicates the next day, and the final three replicates the next day. Prepare a plot of each matrix pair using the undiluted matrix on 1 axis and the 80% matrix on the other axis. Draw vertical and horizontal lines corresponding to the means, and to the 95% and 99% confidence intervals. This makes a grid with a "bullseye" at the intersection of the means, surrounded by two rectangles. The inner rectangle represents the 95% CI and the outer rectangle represents the 99% CI. (A software program, such as MedCalc Statistical Software version 17.9.7 (MedCalc Software bvba, Ostend, Belgium; http://www.medcalc.org; 2017) may be used). Make a 45-degree line intersecting the means and rising from left to right. Now, plot each point. Results should be within the 95% CI centered on the mean. If the results trend along the 45-degree line, this represents day-to-day bias. This bias is acceptable, and will be more evident when comparing multiple laboratory data.

Once you have plots of each matrix, also plot the mean results of all matrices on a single plot. A regression analysis should be linear.

Do this testing for as many, up to nine, matrices as feasible.

COMPARING TWO METHODS IN SAMPLES CONTAINING ANALYTE

For method comparisons between an existing method and a new method, conduct repeatability analysis on each digested/extracted matrix as described previously. Also, analyze the undiluted matrices by the current, or existing, method. Prepare the plots as before, substituting the 80% matrix result with the new method result. If both methods obtain equivalent results, the results should plot within the 95% CI or 99% CI rectangles (Figure 8). In addition, plot the means on another graph and preform a regression analysis. The slope should be near one with an intercept near zero.

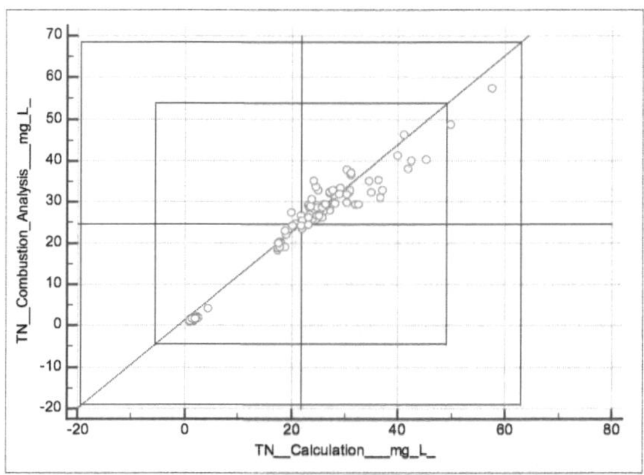

Figure 8 Comparison of two methods using Youden Plot

SINGLE LAB VALIDATION WHEN NO ANALYTE IS PRESENT IN THE MATRIX

Find representative matrices with concentrations near the lowest point of the calibration curve or containing no detectable analyte. Split each matrix into two portions. Spike one of each portion at low, medium, and high points of the curve. Spike the other of each portion at almost the same, but 20% different concentration. Simulate sample transport, storage, and receipt at a laboratory. Perform all checks necessary to ensure samples were "preserved" properly. Document an acceptable range for temperature, ambient light, pH, chlorine, etcetera. Extract or digest each matrix as a real sample. Calibrate the method according to the new method instructions and analyze nine replicates of each portion of each matrix. Do three replicates on one day, three replicates the next day, and the final three replicates the next day. Prepare a plot of each matrix pair using 1 spiked matrix on 1 axis and the 20% different spiked matrix on the other axis. Draw vertical and horizontal lines corresponding to the means, and to the 95% and 99% confidence intervals. This makes a grid with a "bullseye" at the intersection of the means, surrounded by two rectangles. The inner rectangle represents the 95% CI and the outer rectangle represents the 99% CI. (A software program, such as MedCalc Statistical Software version 17.9.7 (MedCalc Software bvba, Ostend, Belgium; http://www.medcalc.org; 2017) may be used). Make a 45-degree line intersecting the means and rising from left to right. Now, plot each point. Results should be within the 95% CI centered on the mean. If the results trend along the 45-degree line, this represents day-to-day bias. This bias is acceptable, and will be more evident when comparing multiple laboratory data (Figure 9).

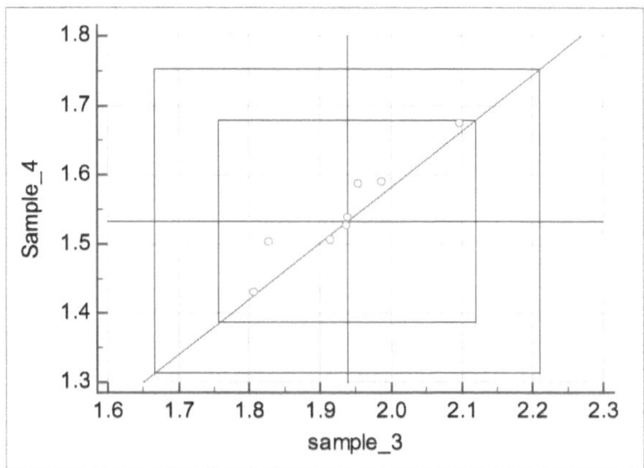

Figure 9 Multiple laboratory data plot showing laboratory bias

Once you have plots of each matrix, also plot the mean results of all matrices on a single plot. Use the known concentration on the x-axis and the found concentration on the y-axis. A regression analysis should be linear (see Figure 7).

Do this testing for as many, up to nine, matrices as feasible. If a matrix fails to line up, there is an interference.

COMPARING TWO METHODS FOR MATRICES WHERE ANALYTE IS NOT PRESENT

For method comparisons between an existing method and a new method, conduct repeatability analysis on each matrix as described previously. Also, analyze the spiked matrices by the current, or existing, method. Remember to take each matrix through all steps, including simulated sampling, preservation, storage, and extraction/digestion. Plot the known concentration versus the means for each method and preform a regression analysis. The slopes should be near equal. If the slopes are significantly different, there is an interference. Repeat for up to nine matrices.

THE OBJECTIVE OF STANDARDIZED METHODS

The main objective of validated standardized methods is to ensure harmonization between laboratory results. To achieve near equal results between labs, you need to use the same methods. If a laboratory makes modifications, these modifications must not change results such that comparisons cannot be made. While each lab validates its own methods internally, the internal validation is not capable of detecting the systematic bias introduced by the variability between analysts, instruments, reagents, and technique. Methods must be significantly rugged so that minor differences between laboratories do not affect results. The method also must be written in an unambiguous manner that clearly points out aspects of the methods a lab should not change. The method must clearly state what matrices it is applicable to and at what concentrations. Sampling and sub-sampling, sample preparation, holding time, digestions/extractions, calibration, analysis, quality control acceptance criteria, calculations, and reporting of results must be defined. If possible, the method should include accuracy and precision data of an example homogeneous, reproducible matrix. Labs can use this matrix to demonstrate that any modification they make, does not affect results.

FULL SCALE COLLABORATIVE STUDIES

Full-scale collaborative studies are expensive and time consuming. In addition, reliable accuracy and precision data is difficult to obtain at low concentrations when the expected random error is 20 - 30% of the mean. Unless the unambiguous written method is already validated by one or two expert laboratories, do not start the collaborative study.

A full-scale collaborative study requires about eight laboratories running five matrices each at a different concentration. The expert laboratories serve as referee labs. Verify method results for each matrix and concentration at the referee labs prior to conducting the study. If a referee lab obtains unsatisfactory results, exclude the matrix from the method, or correct the problem. If you need to modify the method to overcome a problem, repeat the single laboratory validation studies and correct the written method before sending samples to multiple labs.

Many people believe that to overcome the expense of a collaborative study you can use performance evaluation tests. However, these are blind samples sent to laboratories for the evaluation of existing methods. They are not meant to determine the performance of new methods.

Many also think you can evaluate a new method using spiked matrix recovery and precision data. However, if the analysts knows the concentration of the spikes, they unconsciously bias the data closer to the expected value. If the analysts receives the spiked samples as blind concentrations and blind duplicates, the variability is higher. For an unbiased inter-laboratory study, each laboratory should run the same matrices with sample concentrations unknown to the analyst.

CONCLUSION

This has been but a brief introduction into the complex topic of method validation. We need validated methods, for commerce and for environmental testing. Think of all the commodities bought and sold. You expect to know what is in them, and you expect the contents to be correct. Purchasing decisions rely on chemical analysis. Most of these analyses are made using consensus standards. Industry decides what standard to use, and the labs use them. These consensus standards define the analytes, the matrix, sampling procedures, analytical techniques, and required precision and accuracy. The world expects you to follow the standards and judges the correctness of analysis by agreement between labs.

Unlike most commodities, environmental samples expire. You cannot ship environmental samples with short holding times from place to place expecting a tight agreement of results. Environmental samples cannot be stored indefinitely and reanalyzed to settle disputes. No, the correctness of results of an environmental analysis is assumed because you followed the method. It is assumed that if you follow the method, perform the correct quality control, and did not deviate, your results will be the same as anybody else's.

If you modify an environmental method, you must ensure that your results will not differ, in non-interfering samples, from results obtained by the non-modified method. If you are writing a new method, you must clearly define what it does and in what matrices. The method needs to be unambiguous so that laboratories can follow it. All labs who follow it should get results within the precision and bias of the inter-laboratory study.